MW01446539

WE SING!

We Sing! Teaching Kids to Praise God with Heart and Voice

© 2025 by Getty Music Songs, LLC

Illustrations © 2025 by Laura K. Sayers

Published by Crossway
        1300 Crescent Street
        Wheaton, Illinois 60187

All rights reserved. No part of this publication may be reproduced, stored in a retrieval system, or transmitted in any form by any means, electronic, mechanical, photocopy, recording, or otherwise, without the prior permission of the publisher, except as provided for by USA copyright law. Crossway® is a registered trademark in the United States of America.

Cover title design: Jordan Singer

First printing 2025

Printed in China

Scripture quotations are from the ESV® Bible (The Holy Bible, English Standard Version®), © 2001 by Crossway, a publishing ministry of Good News Publishers. Used by permission. All rights reserved. The ESV text may not be quoted in any publication made available to the public by a Creative Commons license. The ESV may not be translated in whole or in part into any other language.

Hardcover ISBN: 978-1-4335-9615-5

Library of Congress Control Number: 2025934012

Crossway is a publishing ministry of Good News Publishers.

RRDS				34	33	32	31	30	29	28	27	26	25
15	14	13	12	11	10	9	8	7	6	5	4	3	2	1

We Sing!

TEACHING KIDS TO PRAISE GOD WITH HEART AND VOICE

WRITTEN BY
KRISTYN GETTY

ILLUSTRATED BY
LAURA K. SAYERS

CROSSWAY®
WHEATON, ILLINOIS

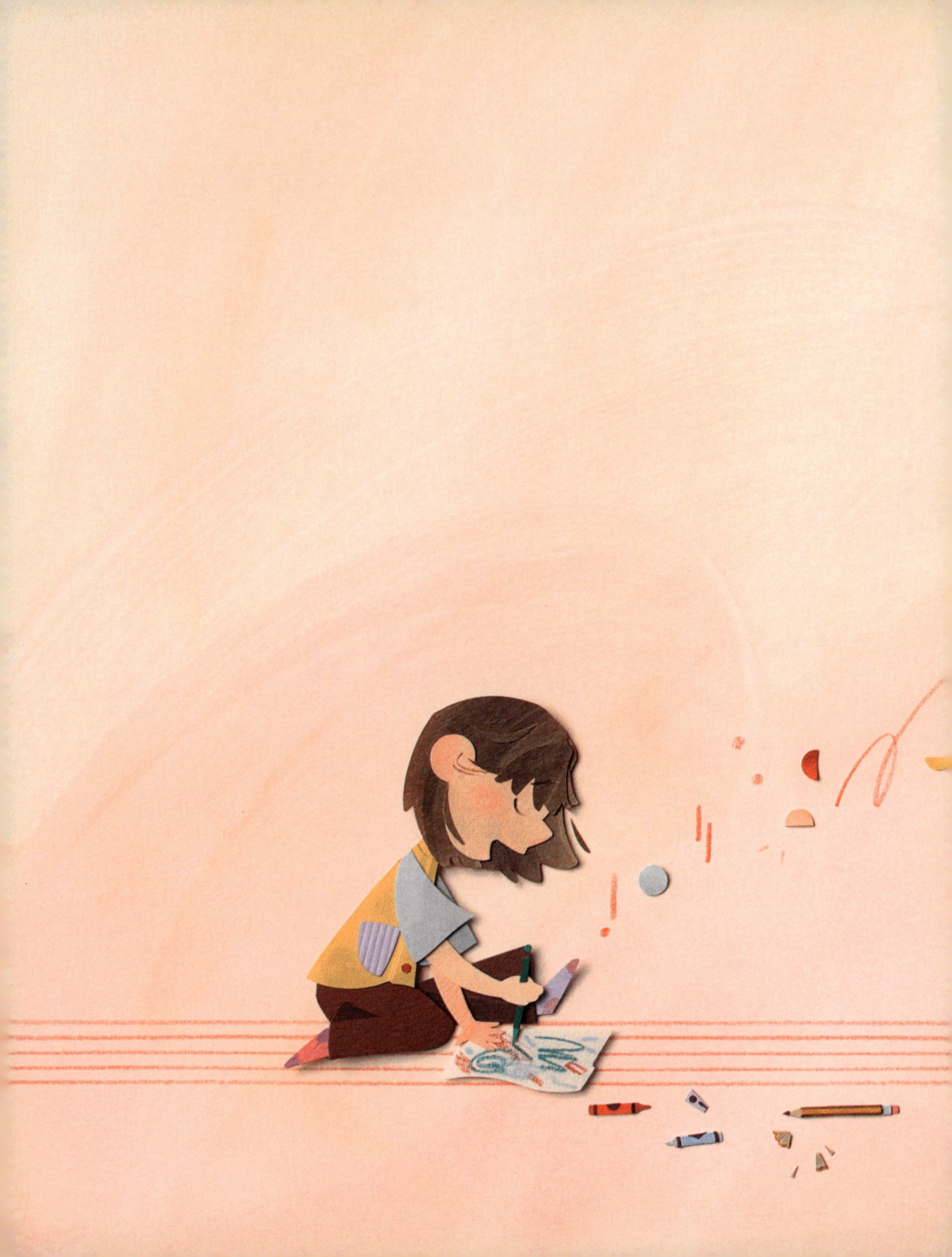

What do you find
beneath your chin?
A music box
your breath fills in
to send out sounds
into the air
that all join up
in songs to share.

Who made your voice,
this great design?
The Lord made yours,
the Lord made mine.
And he delights
to hear us sing,
the one who has
made everything.

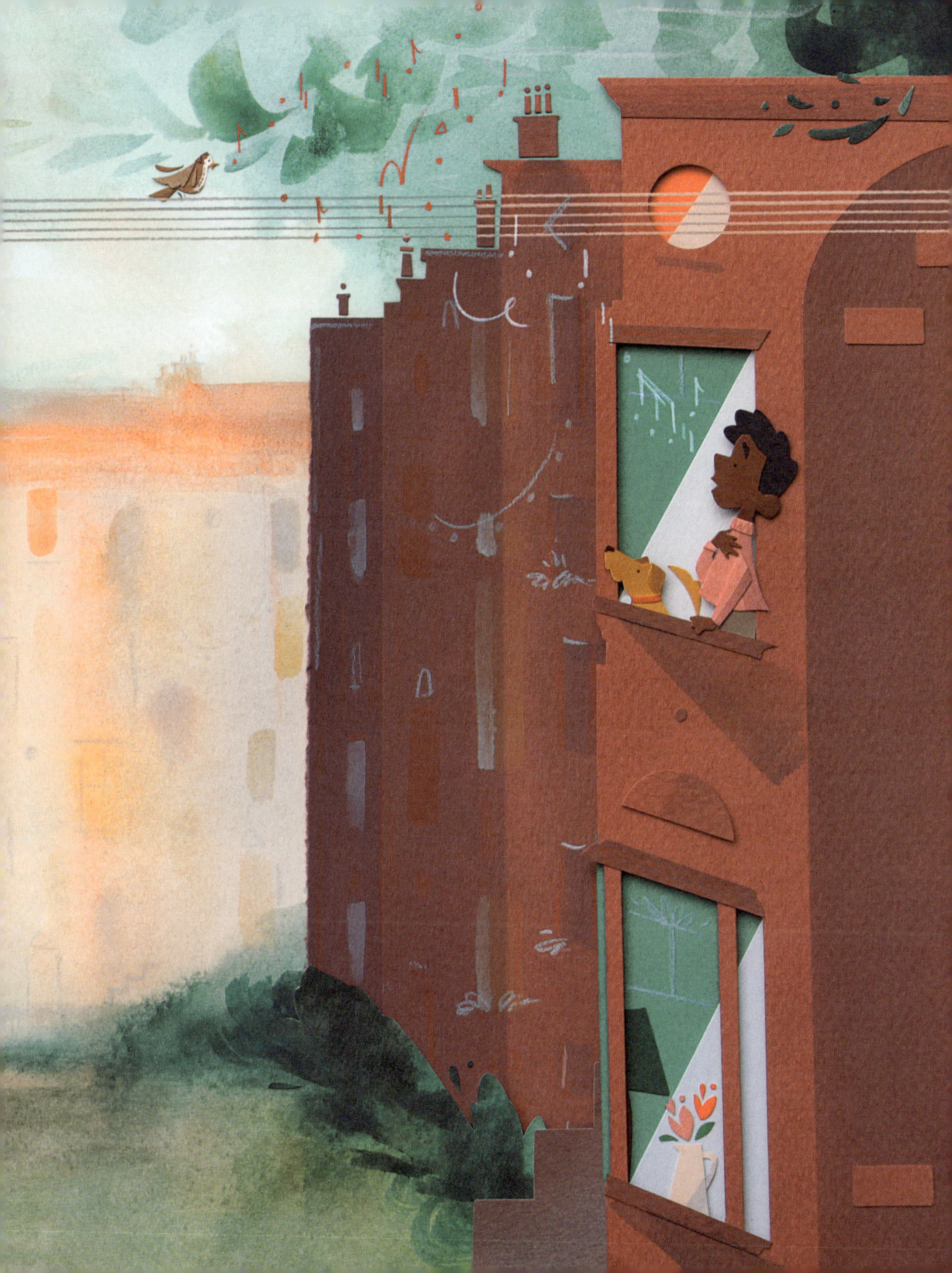

So gather in,
all girls and boys.
Bring singing gifts
of joyful noise
to praise the Lord
so glorious
and true and kind
and marvelous!

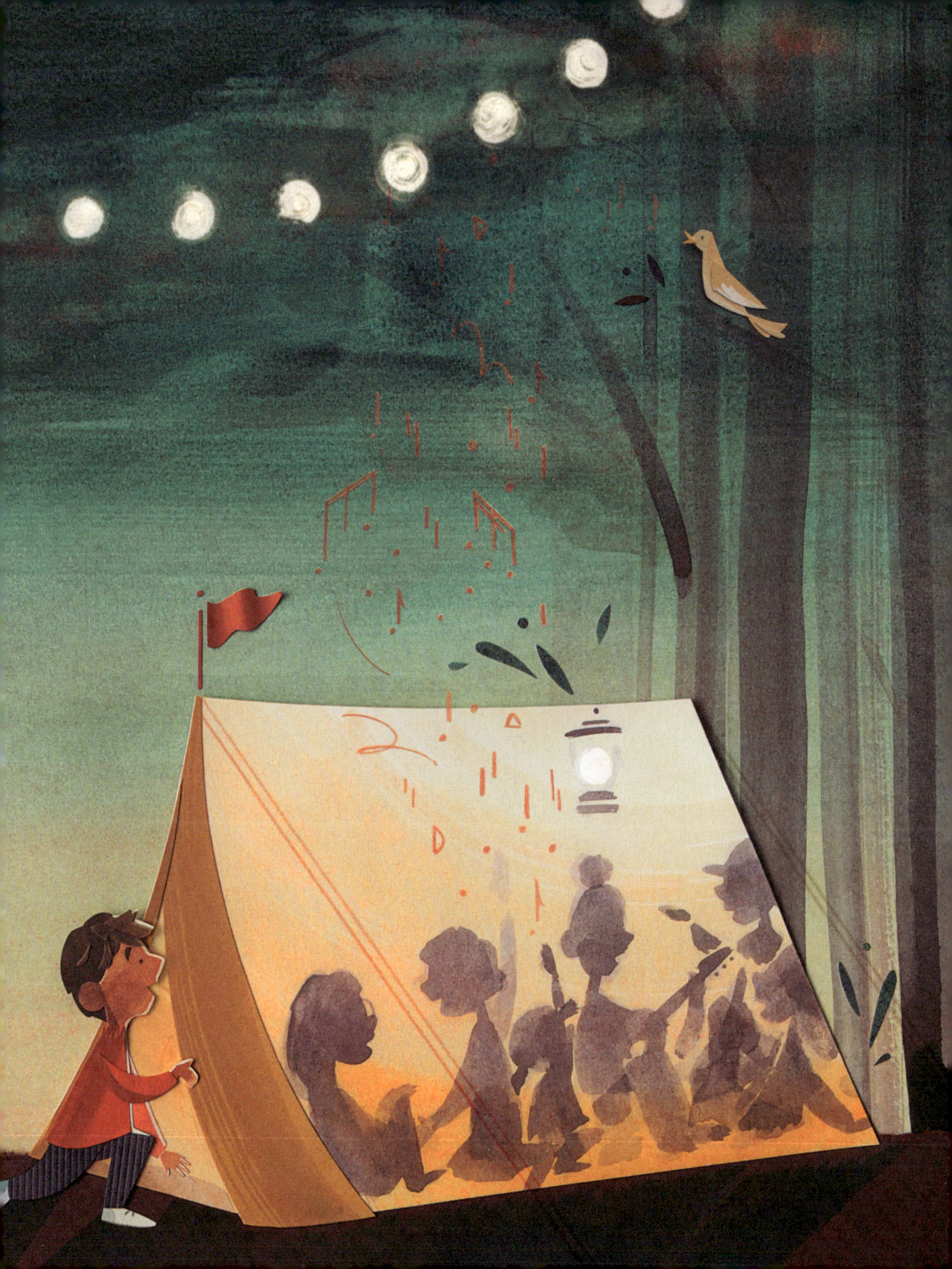

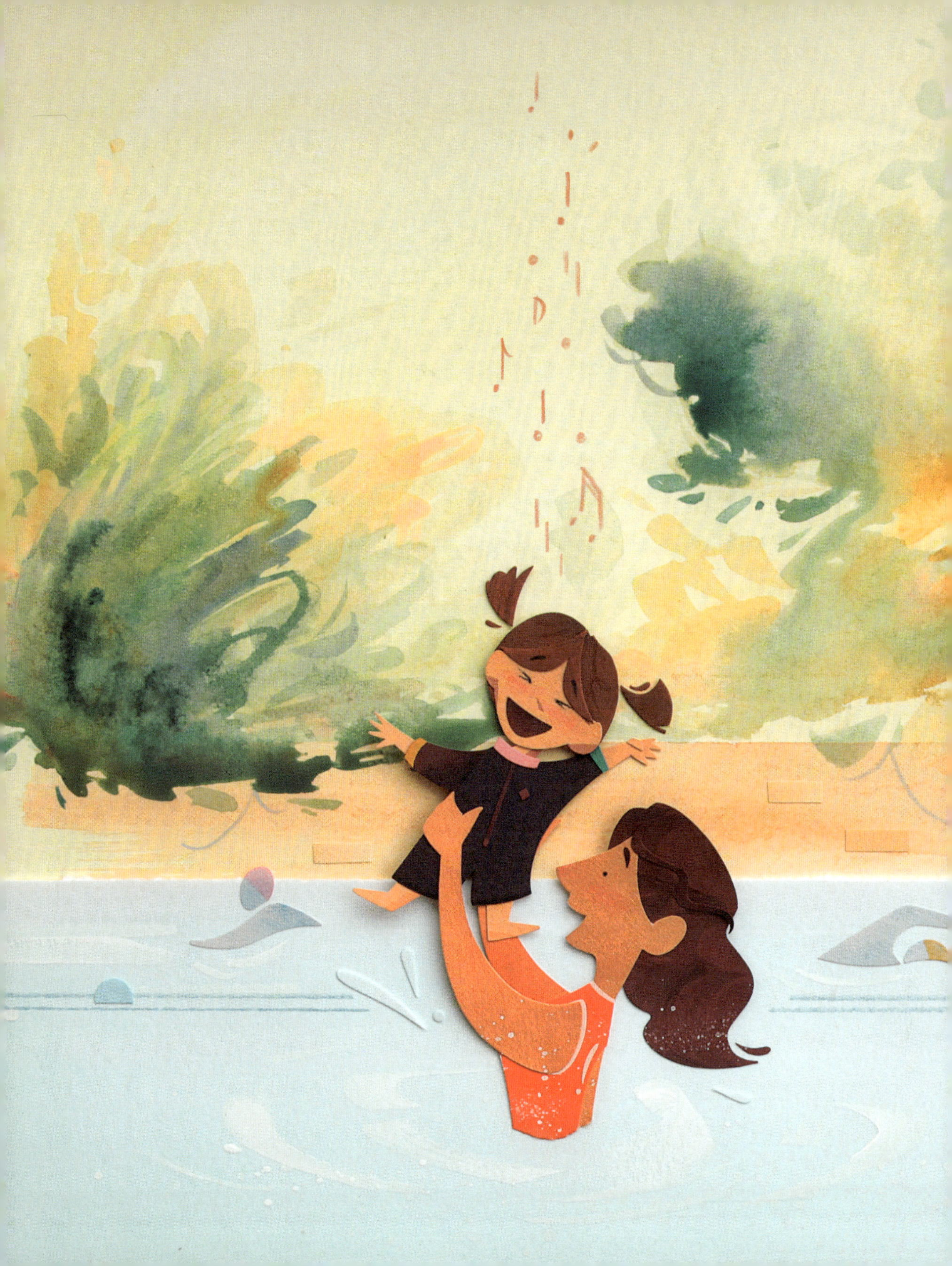

He welcomes us
in Jesus' name;
the Savior takes
our sin and shame
so we can sing,
with hearts made new,
to him who first
loved me and you.

Some people love
to sing out loud,
while some are scared
to make a sound.

Sometimes it's not
your favorite thing,
or when you're sad
it's hard to sing.

But we're still called
to sing our part:
to praise our King
with all our heart.

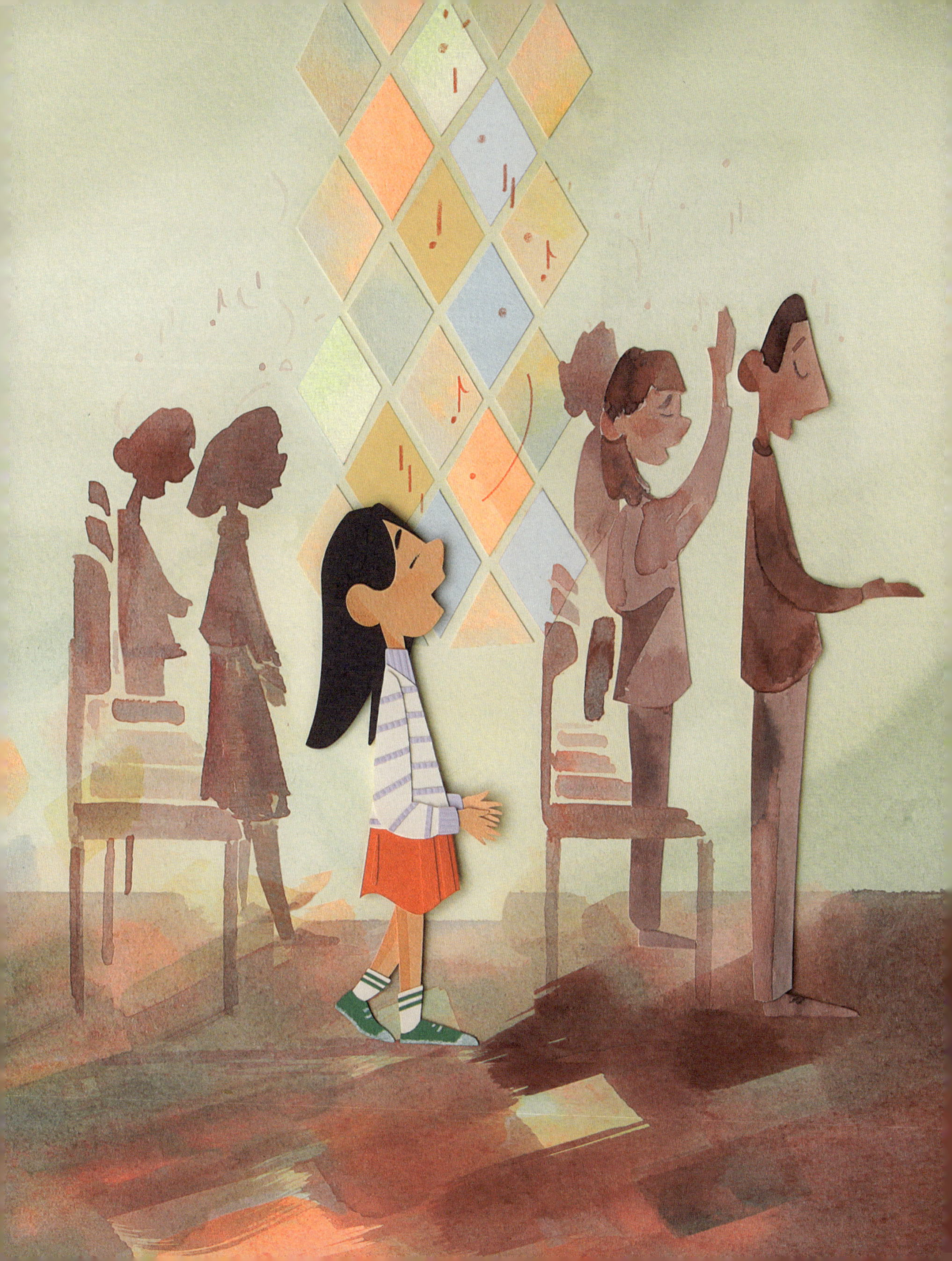

The Bible is
our treasure chest
filled up with words
that are the best

to set with tunes
we like to hear,
and we can sing
year after year.

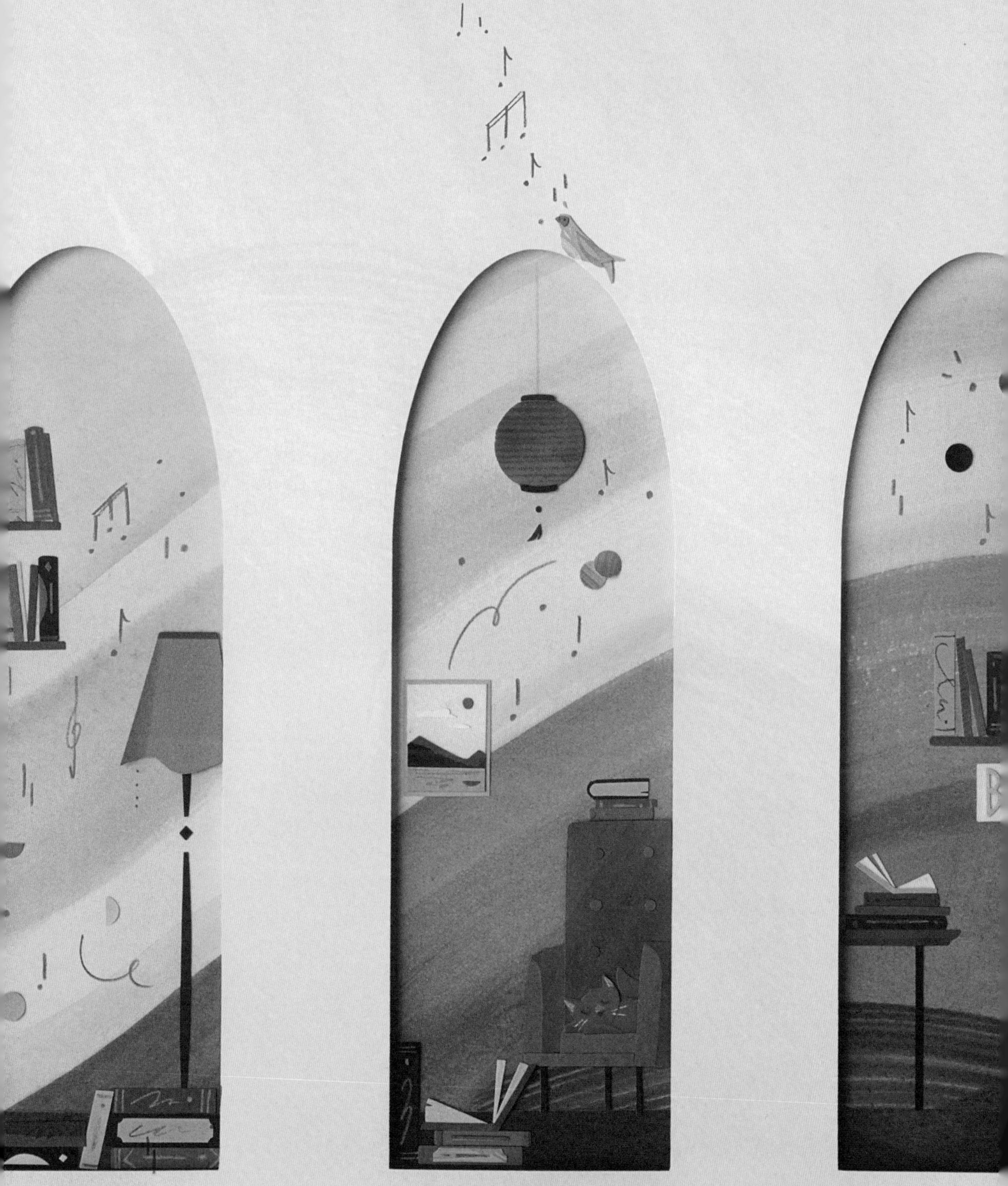

For when we sing
God's truth each day,
we learn it in
a special way.

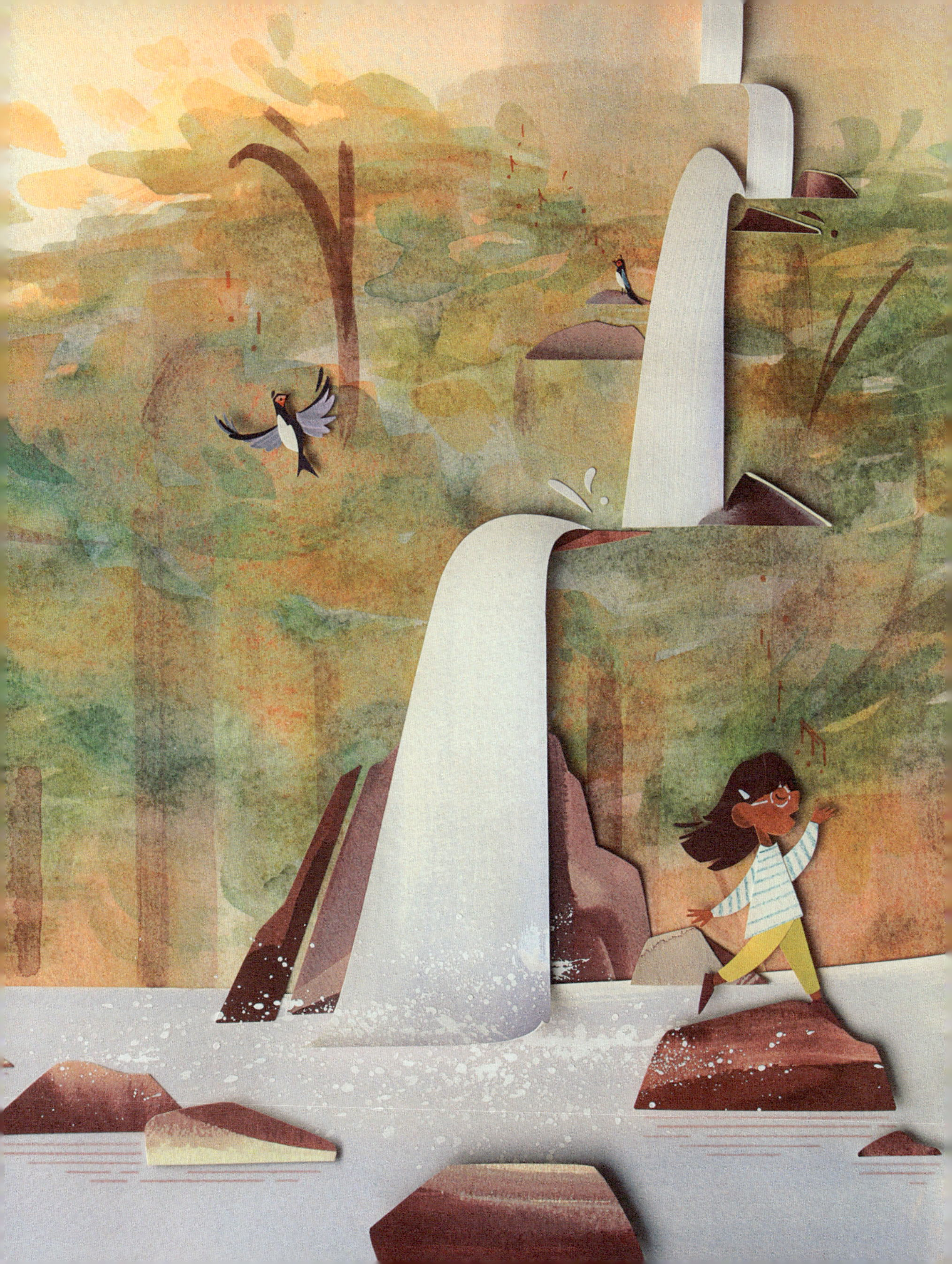

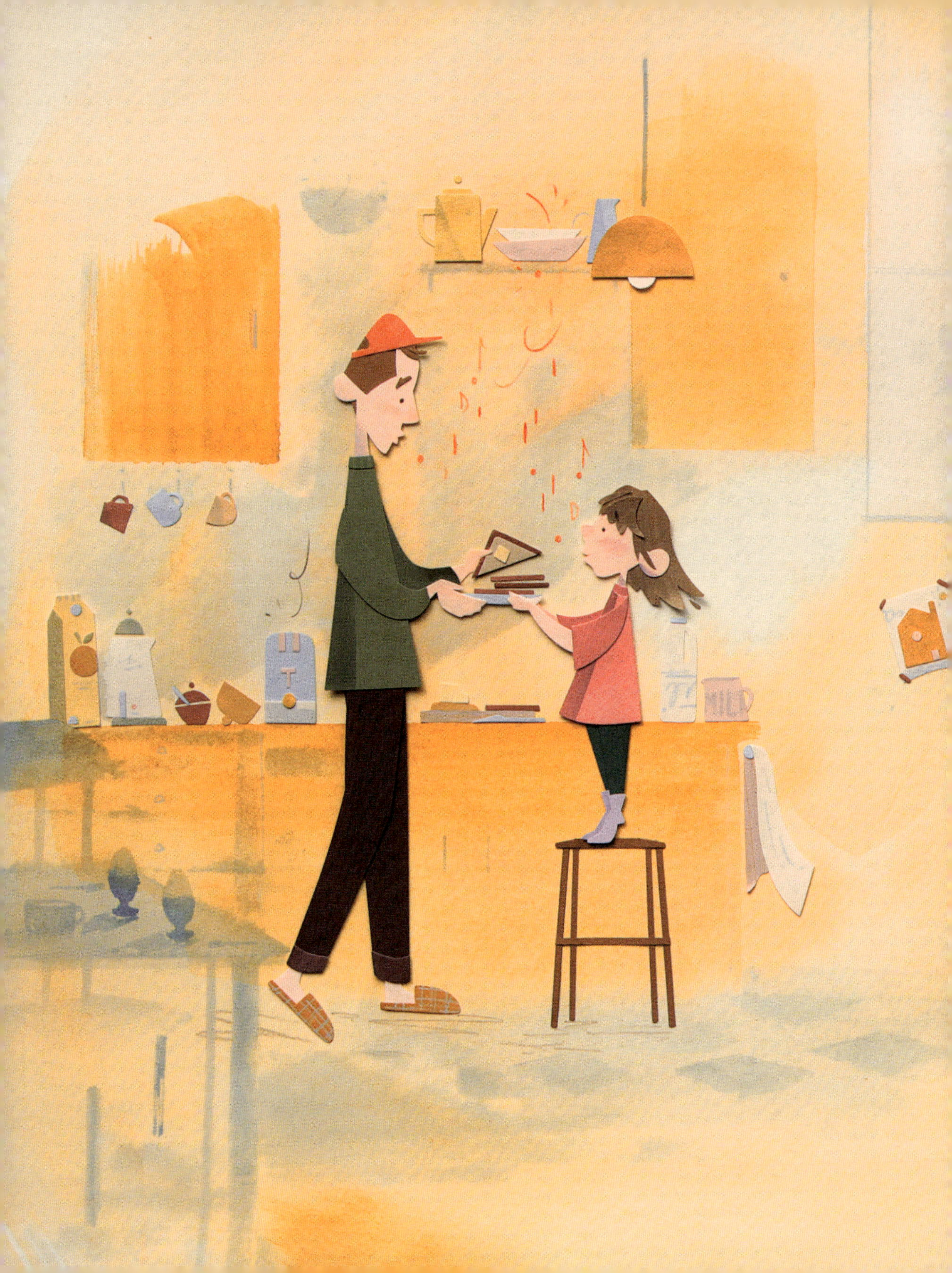

We sing his words
to shape our thought;
songs help them stick,
and so we're taught
to love his truth,
and know his ways,
to hear his song
fill all our days.

Our songs help teach
us how to pray.
They help us find
good words to say
to God (who is
our friend and King)
and then to all
who hear us sing.

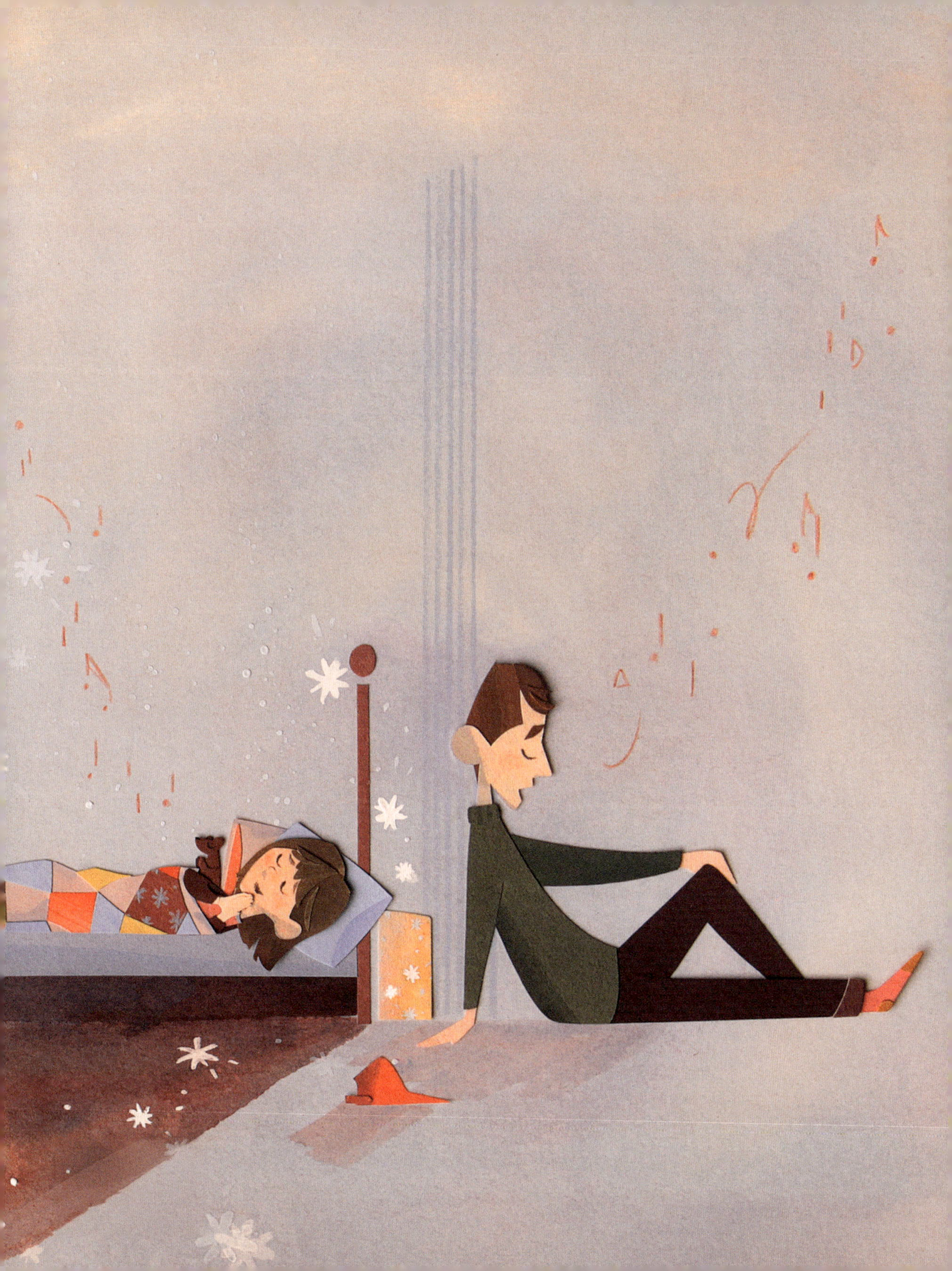

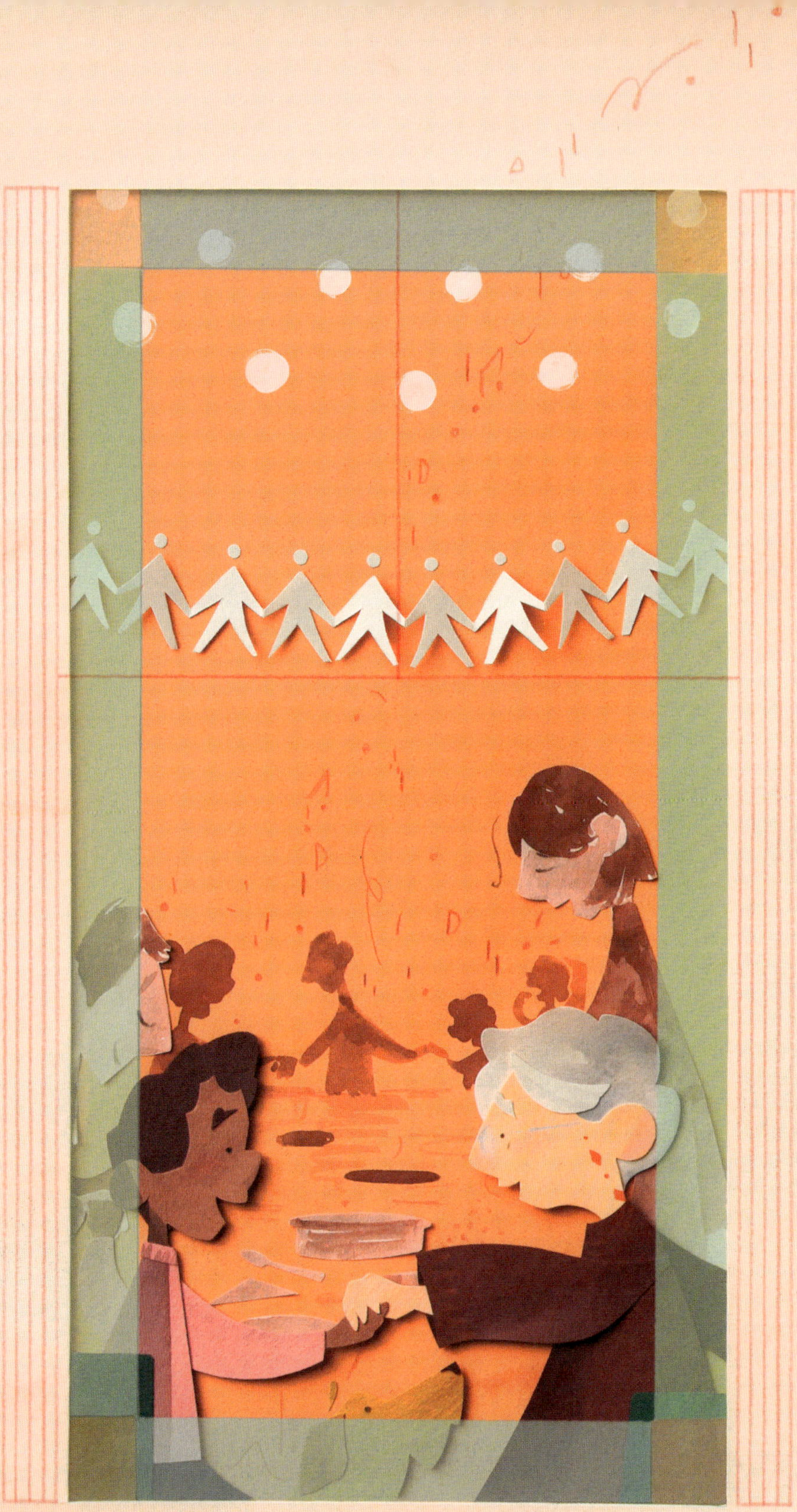

Our voices join,
like linking hands,
with all God's family
from all lands,
with saints who walked
on earth before,
with angel choirs
our praises soar.

We sing God loved
this world and gave
his only Son
that he might save
all those who would
believe his name.
What good, good news
our mouths proclaim!

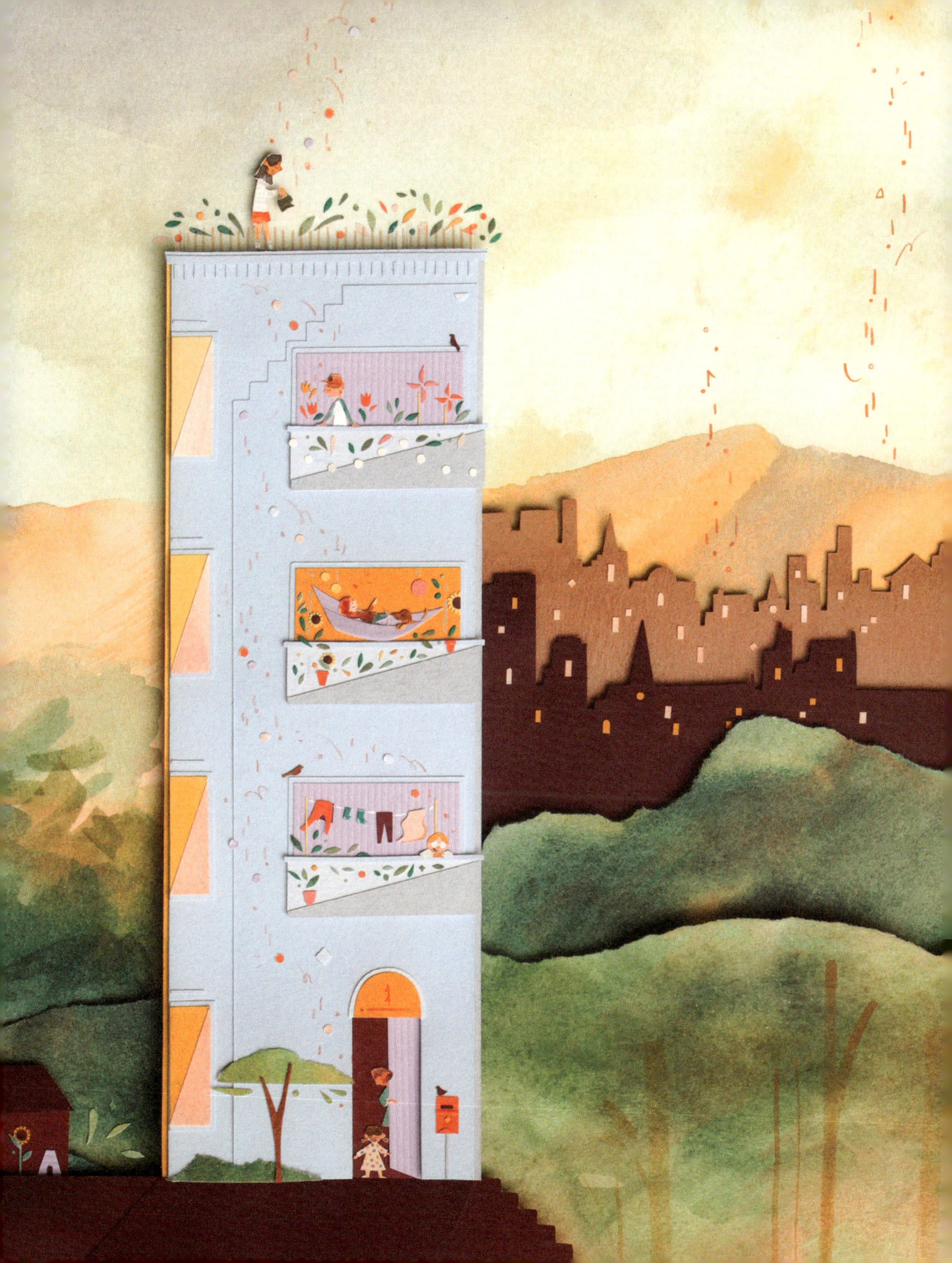

So lift your voice,
each girl, each boy,
until the earth
brims full with joy.

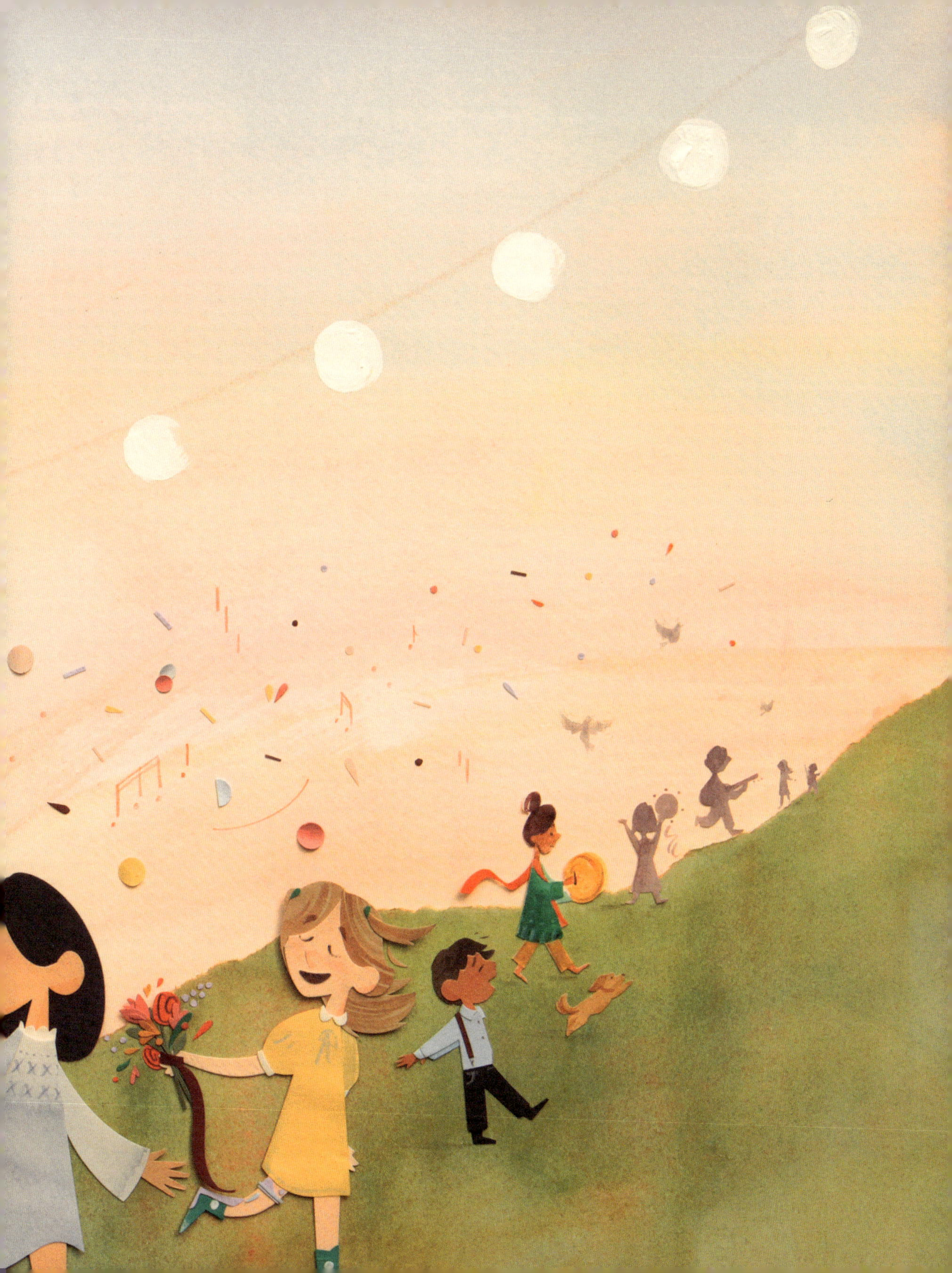

Then what a sound
we all will bring
to heaven's streets
before the King!

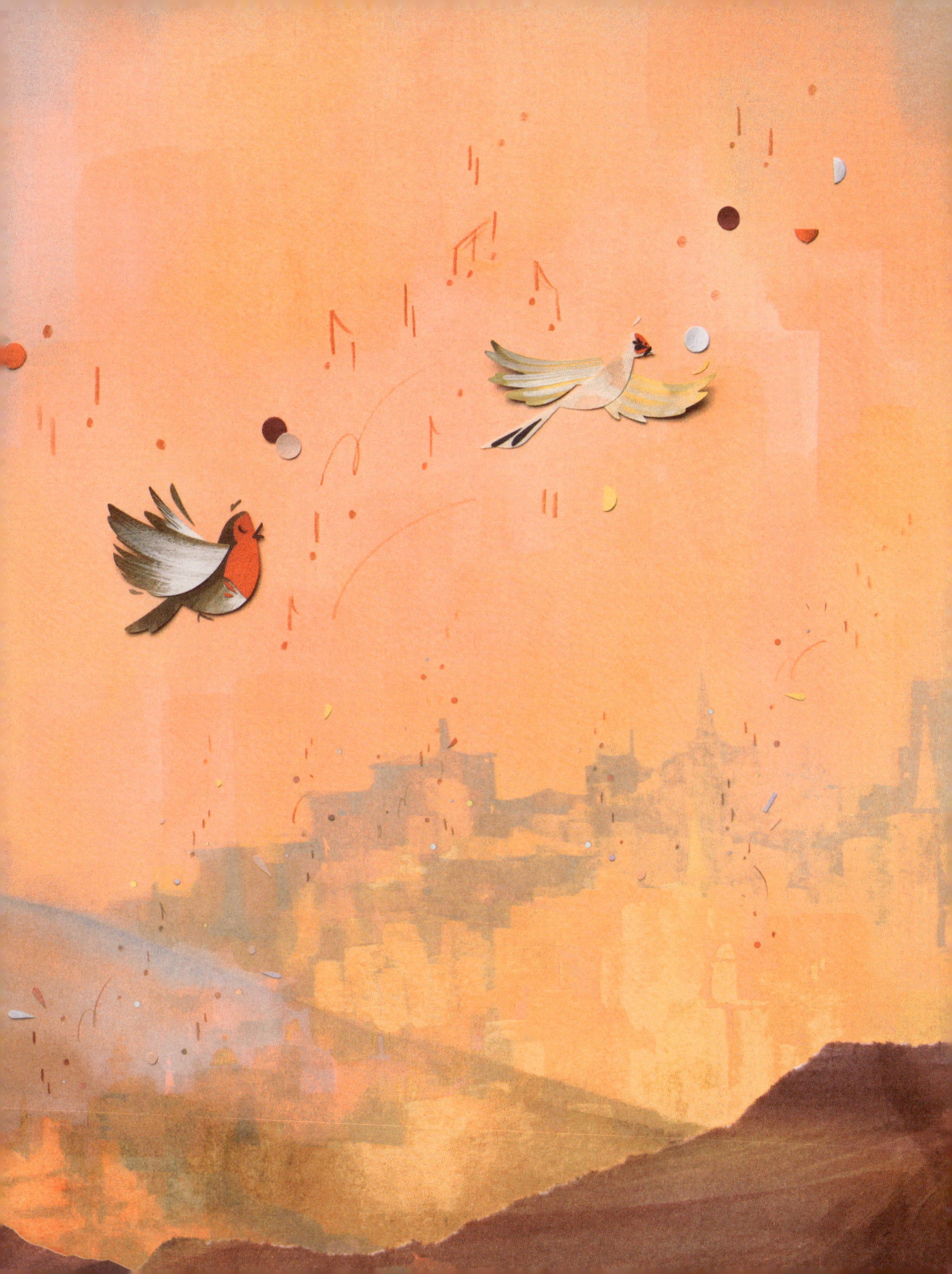

NOTE TO FAMILIES

As a parent, I want my children to know this truth: *Singing is for everyone* (Eph. 5:19). What an incredible gift from God! We bring God praise and honor by singing together to him. But it also brings so much good to us. God has created us to sing. He designed our bodies to be able to sing; he created music as a way to help us better remember the words we sing; and he's made singing as a good way to show how we're joined together with other Christians. So whether it is our favorite thing or not, or whether we are good at it or not, we still sing praise to God. We read his word, we pray his word, we sing his word. It's what we do as his people. And the gospel story gives us the greatest reason to sing. When we consider all he has done for us, the price paid for our sin, and the life and hope we now have, our hearts are moved to sing! Songs voice our thanks, form our prayers, and send out God's truth to others.

It's also important for one generation to pass along to the next that *singing is for every day* (Ps. 96:2). Our songs help inspire our praise through joyful times and even through difficult ones.

Singing is one way we pass along the good news of the Lord—from person to person, whether old to young or young to old. Singing the gospel also helps us recall its truths through the moments of the day: when we wake up, as we work and play, as we travel, as we share meals, and as we go to sleep at night. It also gives us words to share with our friends who need to hear the gospel. And, during the week, we increase our appetite for the feast on Sunday, when we all get to sing together.

And although families change over the passing of years, *singing is forever* (Rev. 19:7). One day, all God's people will gather together—from every generation and from every part of the world—to sing in the great wedding of the Lamb. The very last song lyric noted in the Bible is a wedding song. It's recorded in Revelation 19:6–7:

> Then I heard what seemed to be the voice of a great multitude, like the roar of many waters and like the sound of mighty peals of thunder, crying out,
>
> > "Hallelujah!
> > For the Lord our God
> >   the Almighty reigns.
> > Let us rejoice and exult
> >   and give him the glory,
> > for the marriage of the Lamb has come,
> >   and his Bride has made herself ready."

The Lord is the groom and the church is his bride, and the great feast of that wedding day will be filled with praise from all the family of God. It will be louder than all the great waterfalls of earth and all the thundering storms that have ever been. Millions of people will be in that choir.

I cannot wait for that day. I became a Christian when I was four years old. I prayed that Jesus would be my Lord and Savior and greatest friend. And still he is! Through my life so far, singing has helped me delight in and understand the Lord more deeply. And I know this will be even greater in heaven. Until that day, I pray I will sing to the Lord all the days of my life. I pray you will too.